An Ever-Present
Help in Trouble

NORTHWESTERN PUBLISHING HOUSE
Milwaukee, Wisconsin

All Scripture quotations, unless otherwise indicated, are taken from the Holy Bible, New International Version®, NIV®. Copyright © 1973, 1978, 1984, 2011 by Biblica, Inc.™ Used by permission of Zondervan. All rights reserved worldwide. www.zondervan.com.

The "NIV" and "New International Version" are trademarks registered in the United States Patent and Trademark Office by Biblica, Inc.™

© 2021 WELS Christian Aid and Relief

Published 2022 by Northwestern Publishing House
N16W23379 Stone Ridge Dr.
Waukesha, WI 53188-1108
1-800-662-6022
www.nph.net

ISBN 978-0-8100-3208-8
ISBN 978-0-8100-3209-5 (e-book)

22 23 24 25 26 27 28 29 30 31   10 9 8 7 6 5 4 3 2 1

Preface

Reliability. We appreciate it in our cars and computers. We expect it in our spouse and loved ones. When a friend says, "I'll be there for you," we want our friend to actually show up.

Look at the photo on the front of this little book. Could anything be more reliable than the sun? Unless you are near the north or south pole, every day for your entire life the sun has risen in the morning and set in the evening. You can set your clock by it. In fact, we do. The sun is utterly reliable.

So is our God. The psalmist wrote, "God is our refuge and strength; an ever-present help in trouble" (Psalm 46:1). God never fails to show up. He is always there. In good times and bad, when there is plenty and when there is poverty, in days of peace and days of disaster—God is there protecting us, providing for us, and loving us, especially through his Son, Jesus Christ.

You may be going through a hard time right now. Maybe your plans have been disrupted, your world turned upside down, you need counseling, are alone or grieving. Maybe everything is a mess.

We pray this little book of devotions will bring you a measure of calm in the chaos. It is not filled with clever advice to reduce stress, nor relaxation techniques to lower your blood pressure. Instead, it is filled with the words and promises of a gracious God, a God who loves you so much he sent his only, dear Son to die for you—all so that you could have the peace of forgiveness and the hope of eternal life.

If you find the contents of this book helpful, look at the inside cover. The church family listed there would love to tell you more about God's promises and the peace those promises bring. They'd love to tell you more about the Savior. Get in touch with them. If no church is listed there and you are looking for a good church in your area, go to wels.net, click on "Find a Church/School," and do an easy search.

In the meantime, enjoy these brief devotions. May they calm your heart and strengthen your soul. May they help you see that God is your ever-present help in trouble.

List of Authors

The following pastors provided the devotions contained in this book: Jacob Behnken, Patrick Freese, Robert Hein, Kelly Huet, William King, Bruce Marggraf, Caleb Schoeneck, Daniel Sims, Thomas Spiegelberg, and Richard Warnecke.

Special thanks to Christian Aid and Relief for this booklet's content. For more information or to support Christian Aid and Relief, go to wels.net/serving-others/Christian-aid-relief.

God is our refuge and strength, an ever-present help in trouble. (PSALM 46:1)

ALWAYS THERE

A day at the carnival should be fun, and the little boy was smiling. But he was also scared. He desperately wanted to go through the haunted house, but was a little too nervous to do it by himself. So, he begged his dad to go with him. They walked in together, hand in hand. Every time a scary monster jumped out, the little boy screamed with delight. Afterwards, the boy talked excitedly, and the dad laughed as he shook his sore hand. His son's nervous white-knuckle grip had made quite an impression.

Even though he was scared, the boy was able to go into the haunted house because his dad was with him, holding his hand. His dad's presence gave him the confidence to face his fear.

There are a lot of things in this broken world that scare us: The loss of a job. A relationship on the rocks. Crime. Disease. Disaster. Death. Sin brings all these troubles into our world. Our own sins cause hardship and heartache in our lives. But God is our "ever-present help in trouble." He is with us every step we take through this dangerous world, holding our hand, watching over us night and day.

He has already defeated the greatest danger that faces us. He sent his Son to die on the cross in our place and pay for all our sins. "It is finished," Jesus said from the cross. Every sin has been paid for in full. Our sins no longer condemn us. Satan can no longer accuse us. Death cannot win. Jesus defeated them all. His resurrection from the dead proves it!

The same God who did all this for us, promises to be with us, to strengthen us, protect us and provide for us—even in our most difficult days. As he holds your hand, you can face your fears. God is always there for you.

Heavenly Father, give me peace in your presence
and courage to face my fears.

Amen.

I lift up my eyes to the mountains—where does my help come from? My help comes from the LORD, the Maker of heaven and earth. (PSALM 121:1,2)

OUR GREAT HELPER

Security was tight. The president was scheduled to speak for Memorial Day ceremonies at Arlington National Cemetery. After passing through two metal detectors, spectators had to submit to a pat down and bag search. Uniformed officers were everywhere. Heavily armed Secret Service agents in dark suits were scattered throughout the crowd. Two-man sniper teams took their places on the roofs of each building. The president arrived in his armored limo, affectionately nicknamed "The Beast," and was ushered to the podium by guards on high alert. Every effort possible was made to protect him. No expense was spared, no detail left to chance. Humanly speaking, no one is better protected than the president of the United States.

Friend, be comforted! You are just as well looked after—actually, even better! The One who watches over you is not just a highly trained Secret Service agent or a dedicated law enforcement officer. The One who watches over you, the One who helps you in times of trouble, is none other than the Lord himself, the almighty Maker of heaven and earth.

Just think of that. He called the universe into existence by the power of his Word. He sustains his creation by that same mighty Word every single day. The Creator, who called light and matter into existence out of nothingness, is the same one who protects you and provides for you every single day.

And that's not all. This Creator-God is not just almighty. He is full of compassion. He saw the desperate state of humankind. He saw our sin and brokenness, and he acted. He sent his Son, Jesus Christ, to die on the cross for our sins. His precious blood has washed away all your sins. God forgives you.

Lift your eyes up to him, and trust in the help of his mighty power and compassionate heart every day.

Mighty God, merciful Father, help me.

Amen.

"In this world you will have trouble. But take heart! I have overcome the world." (JOHN 16:33)

TAKE HEART!

Good things come to those who wait. When God closes a door, he opens a window. Time heals all wounds. Just think about how much worse other people have it. It is what it is.

Those are all examples of platitudes, statements that are intended to be helpful and encouraging but aren't. Another example, "Everything is going to be okay." Usually, these words are spoken to someone who has experienced a crisis or a loss. The intent is to make the person feel better. But why is everything going to be okay? No evidence is given to support that statement. It seems like a nice thing to say, but really, it's meaningless.

Jesus did not speak in platitudes. Every word he spoke is full of meaning. He was a realist when he said to his followers: "In this world you will have trouble." Jesus didn't sugarcoat it. He gave it to us straight. This world is full of sin. We are all full of sin. The sin around us and in us makes a mess. This world is a mess. Natural disasters. Terrorism. War. Crime. Disease. Death. Our lives are messy. Anger. Broken relationships. Dishonesty. Greed. Selfishness. Immorality. Sin brings trouble. Sin poisons our world and our lives.

But Jesus is the antidote to sin and all the trouble sin causes. He said, "Take heart. I have overcome the world." How? By living a perfect, sinless life in the place of every sinner. By going to the cross and shedding his priceless blood as the payment for the world's sin. By rising from the dead to secure a better world for us, the perfect peace of heaven.

Dear friend, take heart! The world is a mess. Your world is a mess. But Jesus has overcome the mess. Jesus has conquered sin and Satan. And his victory is your victory, now and forever!

Thanks be to you, O God. You give us the victory through our Lord Jesus Christ.

Amen.

We know that in all things God works for the good of those who love him, who have been called according to his purpose. (ROMANS 8:28)

WORKING FOR OUR GOOD IN ALL THINGS

Justin couldn't believe it. He was sitting in the emergency room. He had slipped on piece of ice and landed awkwardly on his right arm. It was broken. Now he wouldn't be able to play in the regional playoff game at Western High on Saturday night. What rotten luck!

Then the doctor came over, with a funny look on his face. "Your arm is broken, but we also need to do some more tests." A week later Justin was undergoing treatment for the cancer those tests discovered in his arm. They caught it early. He was going to be okay. And to think, they never even would have known he had cancer if not for the "rotten luck" of breaking his arm.

This story illustrates a basic truth about our God: He can turn bad into good for his people.

Right now, you are going through a rough time. The destruction and disruption caused by a disaster are life changing. Disasters are bad. But God can turn bad into good. How many blessings have you already seen in recent days brought by the disaster? Volunteers helping to clean up. Strangers sharing a meal. Neighbors helping neighbors. God can make good things happen even during such a tough time.

The ultimate example of God turning bad into good happened 2,000 years ago just outside the city walls of Jerusalem. There the Son of God was nailed to a cross for sins he did not commit. It was a great injustice. But God turned that bad into good. Because Jesus died on the cross, we don't have to. Because Jesus took our punishment, God doesn't have to punish us. Instead, we have God's forgiveness and friendship.

This is a bad time, but remember—God is working for your good. Why? Because he loves you. And he always will.

Lord, help me to trust that in all things you are working for my good.

Amen.

He will command his angels concerning you to guard you in all your ways. (PSALM 91:11)

BODYGUARDS FROM GOD

Secret Service agents go through years of training in the hope to serve. Only after successfully completing this rigorous training do they get the opportunity to put that training into practice. After all, they have to be the best because their job, the one they swear to carry out at all costs, is to protect the president of the United States.

What if we, like the president, had Secret Service agents guarding us? Wouldn't we feel safe? The truth is, we have something better.

God promises that his angels watch over us. No matter where we are, what we encounter, or what difficulties we face, God promises that with his command he has dispatched his mighty angels to watch over our ways. Far more powerful than any human bodyguard, far more able to keep us safe from harm, these agents of our God are always with us.

Why then, we might wonder, do we still encounter difficulties or even disasters? In sending his angels, God isn't promising a complete absence of trouble in this life. In fact, he tells us we can expect trial and tribulation in this fallen world. In the midst of those troubles, however, he promises that he is still sending his angels to guard and keep us, often likely in ways that go unnoticed. We can take comfort in the protection of God's angels in every circumstance we face.

Best of all, we know what those angels who guard our ways now will one day do for us. We can know that because God has given us his Son Jesus to be our Savior, because he has freed us from our sins with his perfect life and innocent death in our place, one day the angels will deliver us to our Savior's side forever. There he will forever free us from all sorrows and trouble.

Heavenly Father, thank you for sending your angels to watch over me.

Amen.

He heals the brokenhearted and binds up their wounds.
(PSALM 147:3)

HEALING FOR THE BROKEN HEART

Doctors and nurses are valued members of society. When we or our loved ones fall ill, they bring help and healing. When illness strikes, we not only rely on their expertise, but also appreciate their kindness and reassurance.

How can we heal from a broken heart? No doubt, mental-health professionals serve an important role and can bring about great good for many individuals. No doubt, families, friends, and support groups can also help us overcome the injury of a broken heart.

At the same time, emotional wounds don't heal in quite the same way as physical ones. While physical injuries might leave a scar, with time, the pain tends to go away. Our bodies heal. Emotional wounds aren't always like that. The pain from them can last for months or even years. Sometimes a trigger can cause that pain to flare up without warning.

What a comfort God gives us when he tells us that he heals our broken hearts. With his almighty power, he can accomplish what for us would be impossible. When we feel our hearts break, when the wounds are fresh on our souls, we can look to him for healing that only he can give. We can rely on his promise that he heals the brokenhearted.

We can have such great confidence in him because when we were in our greatest need, he gave the healing that only he could. With the blood of his dear Son Jesus, poured out for us on the cross, he took away all our sin and healed our sin-sick hearts. Through believing in Jesus, we have healing from sin and death and are now restored children of God.

And so, in all our hurts on this earth, no matter how great, we can trust that in his boundless love for us, he is always ready to bring comfort and healing.

Heavenly Father, when I am hurting, heal me. Bind up my wounds with the healing power of your love.

Amen.

The angel said to them, "Do not be afraid. I bring you good news that will cause great joy for all the people. Today in the town of David a Savior has been born to you; he is the Messiah, the Lord." (LUKE 2:10,11)

GOOD NEWS

Perhaps you remember a time in your childhood when you felt afraid. You felt so much fear, but then, your mother or father wrapped you up in their arms and assured you everything was going to be okay. Your fear subsided.

When we're young, we tend not to demand proof of our parents' assurance that everything is going to be okay. We simply take them at their word. As we grow and mature, chasing fear from our hearts often becomes a more difficult task because we begin to demand proof. "How do I know it's going to be okay?" we want to know.

God wants us to take him at his word. He tells us faith is assurance of what we do not see (Hebrews 11:1), but that doesn't mean God has left us without any proof that everything's going to be okay. In fact, he's given us the greatest proof. He sent his Son Jesus into the world to be our Savior.

We may not often think of it that way, but the fact God sent his Son proves his love. God so loved us that he gave us his only Son. Through his Son's perfect life and innocent death on a cross in our place, he has taken all the wrong things we've done and made us worthy to have eternal life with him.

That good news means you don't need to be afraid. In spite of all the fear you face on this earth, the good news that God loves you, that he is always with you, and that you are safe in his hands is yours. You have the proof: Jesus was born into this world to be your Savior.

Dear Savior, when I am afraid, use the good news of your birth to take away my fear.

Amen.

Cast all your anxiety on him because he cares for you.
(1 PETER 5:7)

RELIEF FROM A HEAVY BURDEN

The metal osmium is the densest known earth element. Just a cup of it weighs more than ten pounds. Imagine having to carry around a bag full of osmium everywhere you go. To call it a burden would be an understatement.

Sometimes, however, we carry around a burden greater than that. The anxieties we feel in our hearts can seem heavier than any physical load. Those anxieties can build slowly over time from the everyday pressures of life, or a disaster can strike in an instant and with it release the floodgates of anxiety.

No matter how our anxieties come to us, no matter how heavy the load, our God says to us, "Let me carry that." He assures us that we and our future are safe in his hands, so we don't need to carry the burden of anxiety. We can cast off our anxiety and entrust ourselves to his gracious, loving care. As much as a sense of relief washes over us when we can release a heavy physical burden, we are even more at peace when we can let go of the anxieties that trouble our hearts!

And that's just what God tells us to do. Of course, that's easier said than done. Our hearts can tenaciously hold on to anxiety even when we know it's not doing us any good. That's why we need the constant assurance that the Lord gives us in this verse from Peter. God cares about us! With greater concern than any earthly father, with more tenderness than any earthly mother, God cares for us more than we can fathom.

God loved us so much he gave us his Son to save us eternally from sin and death. Confident of that, we can be sure he will also care for us in all the other burdens of life.

Heavenly Father, when anxiety burdens my heart, remind me of your love and care. Use that assurance to help me cast all my burdens on you.

Amen.

You, Lord, are a compassionate and gracious God, slow to anger, abounding in love and faithfulness. (PSALM 86:15)

ALWAYS FAITHFUL

Is God trying to get even with me? You probably don't feel this way every day, but when your worst fears come true you can't help but wonder.

Jonah felt he had to run away. God told him to go and preach to a city. Jonah was afraid of the people in this city. He had this deep anger toward the people there. Jonah didn't want them to know God's mercy. He ran away from them. He wanted to run away from God. He got on a boat and sailed as far away from that city as he could.

God caused a storm to stop Jonah. It was a bad storm. Jonah and everyone on the boat felt in danger. Did God cause the storm because he was mad at Jonah? Was God getting even with Jonah?

No. The worst thing for Jonah would have been for him to run away from God. Even through this storm God protected Jonah and the other people on the boat. God had compassion on them. God showed them amazing grace at how he guided them through that storm. God was not angry; he was abounding in love. He was in control even as life seemed to spiral out of control.

You have storms in your life. God is not punishing you. God is not against you. God is not angry with you. God has compassion on you. God loves you. God is faithful and won't break his promises to you. He is always faithful.

And what has he promised you? He promises he loves you so much that he sent his Son to save you. Jesus loves you so much he suffered and died for you. He knows your hurts and your struggles. He promises you that he will fight for you through the struggles and help you in your storms.

Gracious God, help me through the storms I face with your amazing grace. Remind me that you keep your promises.

Amen.

*When Jesus landed and saw a large crowd, he had
compassion on them and healed their sick.*
(MATTHEW 14:14)

ALWAYS COMPASSIONATE

"Why did this have to happen to her?" "Why must he hurt
like this?"

You hurt when someone you love hurts. Have you ever
wished you could take their pain away? You would rather
carry their pain on our shoulders than see them suffer. You
have compassion. But your compassion can only accomplish
so much.

Jesus is different. He is not limited like we are. He sees the
hurt. He has compassion on them. He knows the hairs we
have on our heads. Do you know how many hairs you have on
your head? Unless you have zero hairs, you don't. Jesus knows
everything about us. He knows what hurts and he knows how
to help. He knows the sick. Jesus has compassion on them. As
Jesus once healed the sick, He is still the Great Physician of
body and soul today.

Jesus would endure pain to help those hurting. He gave
his life for those in pain. Jesus promises an end to suffering,
an end that you will see and know in heaven. Jesus rose and
promises that he will even save you from death itself. Before
heaven is your home, he asks for your prayers and promises
to help.

He may heal what hurts right now. If he does not, know
that he will not abandon you in your pain. Jesus' compassion

for you compelled him to rescue you. Jesus is always compassionate, in sickness and in health.

Jesus, physician of body and soul, help me and all the hurting. No disease, illness, or injury is too much for you to bear. Boldly we pray for the sick. Comfort them, for you are our always-compassionate God.

Amen.

For God so loved the world that he gave his one and only Son, that whoever believes in him shall not perish but have eternal life. (JOHN 3:16)

THE BEST GIFT

If you want to give the best gift, you need to love that person who will receive your gift. If you want to give the best gift, you have to know what they need. If you want to give the best gift, you have to sacrifice. You can give a special gift without spending money. But you will have to sacrifice time and effort to pull it off.

To give the best gift you must be moved by love. "God so loved the world." God loves the world, and God loves people in the world like you. God's love for you is personal. Love leads to better gifts. The Christmas gifts you give your family are hopefully better than a gift exchange at work.

To give the best gift you have to know what people need. God knows what we need. He knows we are in trouble. We need this gift so we "shall not perish, but have eternal life." The stakes are high. God does not want you to miss out.

To give the best gift you have to sacrifice. When you don't put thought into your presents, it shows. You see a look in someone's eyes as you get them a new tie. This look says, "Not even close." They are polite, but you know it missed the mark. You didn't take the time to get them something special. God's gift is sacrifice. If our problem could be solved by God giving us a new TV, he could make one out of thin air. God gave you "his one and only Son."

There's only one Jesus. God loves you so much that he gives you his only Son.

The work of the Father, Son, and Holy Spirit makes us daughters and sons adopted into God's family. This is the best gift any of us could receive.

Heavenly Father, thank you for the gift of Jesus
my Savior and the gift of faith to trust
in him as my Savior.

Amen.

May the God of hope fill you with all joy and peace as you trust in him, so that you may overflow with hope by the power of the Holy Spirit. (ROMANS 15:13)

ALWAYS HOPEFUL

Hope can be a flimsy word. You hope it doesn't rain, but it might rain anyway. Some hope almost leads to disappointment. You hope things get better, but you've waited for a while. If we put our hope in things we have no control over, our hopes can feel empty. Hope can be easily replaced with a cynical attitude. That cynical spirit hides joy and peace from us. That cynical spirit makes us slow to trust anyone or anything, even God.

When we put our hope in God's promises, we won't find disappointment. God does not lie. His promises will help us when we suffer and remind that God won us a home in heaven, a home free from suffering.

Even when we are sad, we find joy in knowing that our God cares. He even promises to wipe the tears from our eyes! Even when others hurt us, we have peace through Jesus. Satan wants us bitter and hurt, but in Jesus we find something better. Though God owes us nothing, God is merciful and forgiving. As God has forgiven us, we forgive others so bitterness and hurt do not get the last word in our hearts.

Romans 15:13 begins with hope. Romans 15:13 ends with hope. This is not a hope that will disappoint, because God has the power to do what he promises.

Have you ever had a problem in your life that seemed too big? Sometimes you felt like you had to roll this big problem up a hill. You got tired and sore trying to move that problem along. Sometimes you were afraid you might give up. The Holy Spirit has power. By his power those problems may disappear. No matter what happens his power will help you even in your weakness.

Lord, fill me with hope. Be my strength
when I am weak.

Amen.

Be still, and know that I am God; I will be exalted among the nations, I will be exalted in the earth. (PSALM 46:10)

BE STILL!

Silence isn't always easy for us to maintain, especially when disaster strikes or we face some great hardship in our lives. Our natural response is to question God, to blame him, to demand answers. We expect God to explain to us why he allowed this tragedy to befall us.

But God doesn't promise to explain why he does things the way he does. He doesn't owe us an explanation. And so we search in vain for God's reply. Instead of questioning "why," God calls for humble silence on our part. He insists, "Be still, and know that I am God." Yes, in the face of disaster and earthly loss, we should silently and reverently consider the noble character of our God.

We may not understand why God rules this world the way he does, but we do know his gracious character and trust his goodness. The God who rules the nations is also our God of free and faithful love. He always has our best interest at heart even when we suffer heartache, pain, or loss. He proved his gracious love for us in the gift of his Son, Jesus Christ. We know that God is on our side because he did not spare his dear Son, but gave him up for our benefit. As a result, in Christ, we enjoy the forgiveness of our sins, peace with God and the hope of eternal life in heaven. Having cared enough to meet our greatest need, we can trust God's goodness to us, even in times of trouble.

No, this side of heaven, we won't have all the answers, but we do know where to look for comfort and strength. Rather than questioning God or demanding explanations, there is a better response: Be still, and put your trust in God!

Dear Lord God, in times of trouble, help us remember your name and trust your goodness. Give us peace in the midst of the storm.

Amen.

My flesh and my heart may fail, but God is the strength of my heart and my portion forever. (PSALM 73:26)

GOD, MY STRENGTH

We like to feel we have everything under control in our lives. We like to think we are strong enough to handle whatever comes our way. But then tragedy strikes, and we find we are not in control. In fact, everything is spinning out of control. We are not strong enough to handle this crisis. We are weak and anxious and fearful. It's like we have gotten the wind knocked out of us and don't know how to respond. Yes, our flesh and our heart fail. This makes us feel worse because we think we should be able to deal with this all on our own, but we can't.

Don't despair! The solution is not to make yourself stronger, or try to fix the problem all by yourself. The solution is to look to God and rely on his strength. He will get you through this tough time. Remember when you are weak, he is strong. When you fall, he will pick you up.

Our strength may fail, but God's never will. You can make it through this crisis because God is on your side and promises to bless you, even in times of trouble.

How can you be sure of this? Because not only is God your strength, he is also your portion forever. A portion is an inheritance you have coming to you, blessings you can always count on. God offers you a rich inheritance in Christ. By his perfect life of love and his sacrificial death on the cross, Jesus has won for you the forgiveness of your sins, a place in

God's family, comfort in times of trouble, and the assurance that God is on your side, always working his gracious plan for your benefit. When your heart fails, remember God, your strength and your portion forever!

Lord, when my heart fails and I am in distress, be my Strength, my Rock, and my Deliverer. Help me rest secure in your unfailing love.

Amen.

The Lord your God is with you, the Mighty Warrior who saves. (ZEPHANIAH 3:17)

GOD IS WITH YOU!

We experience many emotions when disaster strikes our lives—heartache, pain, and loss. Perhaps it is the loss of property and possessions, the loss of our good health, or even the loss of a loved one.

That pain can be intense. But there is an emotion even more painful, and that is the thought of abandonment from God. We may wrestle with the feeling that all these bad things happened to us because God is against us. Perhaps he is punishing us for some sin we committed. Perhaps God doesn't care about us. It's bad enough to suffer earthly loss, but to think you have to face this all alone because God is "out to get you" can be a burden too heavy to bear.

When all things seem against you and drive you to despair, cherish this promise from Zephaniah 3:17: "The Lord your God is with you, the Mighty Warrior who saves."

God is not against us. He is for us; he is on our side. How can we be sure of this? Because of God's gift to us of his Son. One special name of Jesus makes this clear. We call Jesus "Immanuel." That literally means "God with us."

Jesus came to us meek and mild as a little baby on Christmas. But don't be fooled by his humble appearance. Jesus is God, our mighty warrior, who came to rescue us from our sins and restore us to a right standing with God. This victory he won for us by his perfect life of love and his sacrificial death upon the cross.

Since Jesus cared enough to meet our greatest need, we also can count on him to help us deal with our earthly pain and loss. Remember that God is always on your side!

Dear Lord God, in times of earthly loss help us remember you are on our side. You care, and promise to help us in our time of need. Help us find comfort in your unfailing love.

Amen.

He who did not spare his own Son, but gave him up for us all—how will he not also along with him, graciously give us all things? (Romans 8:32)

CERTAIN OF GOD'S LOVE

The story is told about a train headed down the tracks toward a bridge that was out. If the train continued on its current path, all the passengers on board would plunge to their death. A father stood next to a switch track. All he had to do was push a button and make that train take a different path; a path which would lead all those passengers to safety.

But there was one catch. On that other track his son was trapped, and couldn't get free. The father faced a heart-wrenching decision. Should he spare his son and allow all the people on board the train to die? Or should he push the button, and sacrifice his son's life to save those people? What a difficult choice that would be!

In reality that's the dilemma God the Father faced. He had to make a choice. Should he keep his dear Son Jesus safe with him in heaven and allow all of us to die in our sins? Or would he be willing to sacrifice his Son to save us? You know the choice God made, for you—"He who did not spare his own Son, but gave him up for us all—how will he not also along with him, graciously give us all things?"

Sometimes we forget that our salvation cost God something. He didn't just snap his fingers. He gave something up. He sacrificed his Son's life to save ours. Here we find positive proof of God's gracious love for us. Remember that during tough times. Remember that when God seems distant from you. God cares. God is always seeking your best interest. God made his choice for you!

Dear Heavenly Father, your love for us is amazing. You gave your best for us. The gift of your Son meets our greatest need. Teach us not to worry about the future, but always rest secure in your unfailing love.

Amen.

Wait for the LORD; be strong and take heart and wait for the LORD. (PSALM 27:14)

HURRY UP AND WAIT

Hurry up and wait! After the initial shock, the hardest part of the days that follow a disaster is the hurry up and wait. I need to do something but I don't know what. Needing to figure things out but not knowing where to start. Needing answers but I'm waiting on this agency or that phone call. Then there are the wonderful people who want to help, but because you don't know the next steps you don't know how to tell them to help.

In these moments when the urgency is overwhelming, hear these words of the LORD from his servant King David: "Wait for the LORD; be strong and take heart and wait for the LORD." David writes this as armies advance, his world is crashing around him, and the pleading for immediate relief is on his lips.

David points us to where our strength comes from when all our strength and emotional fortitude have eroded and we are exhausted and raw. He says, *Wait for the Lord!!* Sit with the LORD who has redeemed and rescued you. Wait, find your strength, hope, and emotional stability in the unchanging one.

This type of waiting isn't like waiting on the insurance company, adjusters, or banks for call backs. Waiting on the Lord is sitting with God, putting your trust in the one who loves you so much he died for you. Waiting on the Lord is remembering his mercy and strength.

Waiting is hard, but when you know the one you are sitting with is the almighty Creator of the universe, you know the wait is worth it. Today it may be tough to read these words. If that's the case, God understands—lay it before him, and trust he is your strength!

Lord, I don't understand, my heart is broken with the losses I've experienced, but I trust in you. Give me your strength, guard my heart, and move me to a place of emotional and spiritual peace as I wait for you.

Amen.

For as high as the heavens are above the earth, so great is his love for those who fear him; as far as the east is from the west, so far has he removed our transgressions from us.
(PSALM 103:11,12)

DEPTH OF LOVE

When was the last time you flew? Ever flown so high that you can actually see the arch of the earth on the horizon? When you get that high, you don't see streets, cars, people, and animals; you don't even see buildings. At most, you may see only outlines.

God uses the illustration of being so high to remind you of the monumental, unshakable, incomprehensible depth of his love for you.

God knows that in the darkest moments, the hardest days, the sleepless nights, that Satan whispers lies to you. Lies that sound something like: "God has abandoned you. God must not love you or none of this would have happened." Or the guilt-ridden lie: "God's punishing you for _____."

Oh, the lies Satan tries to tell! But pause today with the Lord of creation who is truth. He is the One who knit you together in your mother's womb. Listen as he reminds you of the depth of his love. Listen as he reminds you that he isn't punishing you for some sin, but he's already paid for that sin and removed your guilt and shame. He's removed it so far that it is beyond sight and memory. That's his word of hope and grace for you today. He's moved heaven and earth for you. He took on flesh and died for you. He loves you more than you can imagine. His heart breaks for you. And he has not abandoned you.

Heavenly Father, when it's hardest to feel your love, envelop me with your love and protection. Let me experience your love through those you place around me to remind me of your love, especially on the days that it is the hardest. Let me trust in you.

Amen.

*"I know the plans I have for you," declares the L*ORD*, "plans to prosper you and not to harm you, plans to give you hope and a future."* (JEREMIAH 29:11)

RECALCULATING . . .

Think about what happens when you have to drive somewhere you haven't been before. So you say, "Hey Siri" or "Hey Google" and ask for directions. You then blindly follow the directions only to find out that the route is blocked, so you keep going straight. You hear a noise and the app begins "recalculating" to find the next-best solution.

Do you feel like life is "recalculating," like you thought you were headed in the right direction and suddenly are met with a roadblock. Frustrations and anger can fester as the "fastest route" turns out not to be the path that God wants us on at that moment.

Do you feel like God should be like Google or Siri and find us the fastest route with the least traffic or detours? His plans aren't about the quickest or easiest routes. His plans for us are plans that draw us closer to him. Plans that guide our hearts to completely trust in him, and focus on him.

The destination is sure—eternity with him. The recalculations we experience here are often routes necessary to keep us from danger, and to bring us closer to the one who is living, active, and ruling on our behalf. When Jeremiah wrote these words, Israel was in shambles. People were being carried off into exile. The country was falling apart. It would have been easy to despair. But it is here that God says he knows the route and his plans are not for harm, but for our safety and rescue.

Lord, let me trust in your recalculating. Move my heart to follow you and trust that you are working for my good, even though it hurts right now and I'm confused and struggling with all that has happened. Draw me closer to you amid this redirection.

Amen.

"Don't be alarmed," he said. "You are looking for Jesus the Nazarene, who was crucified. He has risen! He is not here. See the place where they laid him." (MARK 16:6)

HE IS NOT HERE

Mary, Mary, and Salome had the worst week of their lives. It started with a parade. The town was in full festival mode. People all around them were partying and carrying on and here they were grieving. Their dear friend was dead. How could the week have taken such a horrific turn of events? Their whole world has come to a crashing halt and it hurt that no one seemed to notice. And just when they thought it couldn't get any worse, it did. Or so it appeared.

Ever been there? Had a week like Mary, Mary, and Salome did, where it doesn't seem like it could get any worse . . . until it does?

His words for you today are the same words the angels spoke to the women, "Don't be alarmed" (literally "stop being emotionally excited"). Emotions are high; you might be holding on by your fingernails, but he tells us we can stop being alarmed and emotionally overwhelmed because Jesus has risen! He did what he said he would do. If he kept the promise, that he would die and rise, then we can trust he's going to keep all his other promises, including the one to "Never leave you, nor forsake you" (Hebrews 13:5).

You are not alone! The risen Christ is ruling on your behalf and is with you in this moment. He knows the darkness, the fear, the worry, the emotions. He says, "I've been there and

I've got you. I conquered death, trust I am holding you right here, right now."

"He is not here!" We need to hear these words of hope and life! Jesus literally has endured the worst of our worst days and has conquered hell, and he is with us today!

Heavenly Father, let the resurrection of Jesus bring me comfort and peace today. Let me trust that because he lives, you got this.

Amen.

Call on me in the day of trouble; I will deliver you, and you will honor me. (PSALM 50:15)

BETTER DAYS AHEAD

There's trouble, and then there's real trouble. The day arrives when trouble seems to come in wave after wave, and some of the waves are so enormous that you wonder how in the world you will survive, or whether life will even be worth living anymore if you do.

Your God has not forgotten you in the day of trouble, and he has not left you to try to survive on your own. Even when hope seems in short supply, God comes to you and speaks to you. "Call on me in the day of trouble," he says. "I will deliver you," he promises. God can take your troubles away, no matter how threatening they seem. God can strengthen you to overcome your troubles, no matter how helpless you feel. God promises to deliver you from trouble, from every trouble, in one of those two ways. And God's promises will never fail you.

But it's even better than that. God makes this promise to you *even though he knows you.* He knows your past, knows everything that you have done wrong, and he knows all your sinful weaknesses. Even so, he still loves you just the way you are. Even so, he gently invites you to call on him and ask him for help. Even so, he promises to deliver you from every trouble.

And God understands trouble. He is no stranger to trouble. God the Son came to earth and was named Jesus. His life on earth was filled with trouble, so much trouble that he died on a cross to deliver you from sin and every trouble.

Jesus overcame a whole world of trouble. He is alive and has promised to do the same for you. Call on him, trust him—there is no higher honor you can give him.

Dear Father in heaven, I need your help. Deliver me from my trouble. Send your Spirit to strengthen me and give me hope.

Amen.

"Though the mountains be shaken and the hills be removed, yet my unfailing love for you will not be shaken nor my covenant of peace be removed," says the Lord, who has compassion on you. (ISAIAH 54:10)

UNSHAKEABLE LOVE

There are times in life when it seems like everything we relied on disappears. Like your whole world falls out from underneath you. Like life's very foundation has been shaken. Times when you wonder, "How can I go on?"

At times like these, it is so very important to know that there is a God who sees and understands. He is the Lord, and his love never fails. No matter how your life has been shaken, his unfailing love for you cannot be shaken. He will work through the pain. He will work through the suffering. And he will work to give you peace.

You can try to do it on your own. "Grit your teeth and bear it," people say. "When the going gets tough, the tough get going." "Just gotta pull yourself up by your bootstraps." Maybe there have been times in your life when relying on your own strength even seemed to work for you.

But then you are shaken to your very core, and your strength drains away. Then it's time to rely on God and his love. The truth is that it's always time to let go of self-reliance and let God's power and strength take over. There is nothing more powerful than God's love for you. His love for you is more immovable than mountains.

His love for you is so rock-solid that he even punished his

own Son, Jesus Christ, for all sin, rather than punishing you. There simply is no force in the universe more immovable, more solid and secure, than God's unfailing love for you.

When you get right down to it, humans are frail, and it isn't difficult to shake us. But not God. His love and compassion will not be shaken.

Dear Lord God, I need your love. Be my rock and my salvation, for Jesus' sake.

Amen.

I consider that our present sufferings are not worth comparing with the glory that will be revealed in us.
(ROMANS 8:18)

A BRIGHT FUTURE

Can you measure suffering? If you were to measure the suffering you're experiencing right now, this minute, on a scale of 1 to 100, how would you gauge it? Would you give it a 20? 50? 105?

How about the glory that will be revealed in you someday; can it also be measured? The Lord says that for believers in Christ Jesus, glory will be eternal and that it's not even worth trying to compare it with present sufferings. In fact, if you could see right now all your future glory next to all your present suffering, your suffering would look puny by comparison.

God is trying to help us to keep our suffering in perspective with this promise. Sometimes we make our suffering worse than it already is because we lose hope. God doesn't want you to lose hope. On the contrary, no matter what kind of suffering you're going through right now, the Lord wants you to be filled with hope as you think about your future.

The reason you can be so certain of future glory in heaven is because God's own Son, Jesus Christ, has achieved it for you. The suffering that humanity deserves because of our sin is eternal; it never ends. But Jesus took that suffering on himself and conquered it on his cross. The Father was so pleased with the sacrifice Jesus made that he glorified Jesus; he raised him back to life and then returned him to his highest throne in heaven. God declared the world forgiven and wants you to believe in Jesus and this promise of future, eternal glory.

No matter how much you're suffering right now, there will be better days ahead—glorious days. No matter how dark life may seem right now, your future is still as bright as ever. That's our hope in Christ Jesus.

Dear Father, only you can give real hope. Fill me with hope for a glorious future in Jesus' name.

Amen.

Do not be anxious about anything, but in every situation, by prayer and petition, with thanksgiving, present your requests to God. And the peace of God, which transcends all understanding, will guard your hearts and your minds in Christ Jesus. (PHILIPPIANS 4:6,7)

PEACE OVERCOMES ANXIETY

A pastor was visiting one of his members in the hospital. She confessed to him that she struggled with anxiety. At that time, her battle was fierce because her husband had just lost his job, so there was a lot to worry about. How would they pay their bills? How would there be any Christmas presents for the children? She said to her pastor, "There is only one place where I have any peace. When I come to church, only then do I have peace."

The peace of God is a great treasure. To know that God loves you for Jesus' sake, to know that God has covered over your sins because of Jesus' perfect life and innocent death—to hear about it in church each week brings a peace that really does transcend all understanding. If only we could always feel true peace! But our anxieties and worries get in the way. There is so much that can go wrong in life. How is it even possible to not be anxious about anything?

We can learn to put our anxieties into God's hands and leave them there. We can learn to open our hearts to him in prayer. We can take God's promise of peace with us when we exit the church doors and keep it with us until we enter again. Life is always looking up when we learn to live this way.

Whether we have learned it or not, it is still true: the peace of God will guard your heart and your mind in Christ Jesus. The peace of God will protect you from every spiritual threat. Let God's peace wash over you in every situation.

Dear Jesus, so often I only see trouble and turmoil. Give me your peace.

Amen.

Jesus said, "I am the resurrection and the life. The one who believes in me will live, even though they die; and whoever lives by believing in me will never die." (JOHN 11:25,26)

CLOSE CALL OR A DIRECT HIT?

Have you ever experienced a "close call"? Maybe you were late because you lost your keys, only to miss an accident ahead of you. You think, "That could've been me!" Or maybe you were in an accident, but if the impact was an inch closer you wouldn't have survived.

We often hope for "close calls" and "near misses." They sure seem better than a "direct hit." But, for as much as it might be nice to avoid disaster, sadly that doesn't always happen. Tragedy strikes and it does not discriminate.

One of life's secrets is that God isn't in the business of close calls. Instead, he does his best work when there's a direct hit. When it comes to the tragedy of evil in life, there isn't a single person who has escaped it. Everyone who is impacted by evil—and everyone is impacted by evil—ultimately will not survive. And that sounds awful—until you hear what Jesus has to say.

Jesus is not the God for those who were lucky enough to get out of harm's way. Jesus is the God for those who have absolutely nothing left—not even their lives. That's why Jesus says he is "the resurrection and the life." Jesus is at his best in situations when people have been hit the hardest, even by death. That's because he knows a thing or two about death. He took a direct hit when he died on the cross. Three days later, he rose from the dead and promised that whoever believes in him will also rise and live with him forever in heaven.

Dear God, thank you for helping me not only in life's close calls, but especially with the promise of your forgiveness as I have suffered a direct hit by evil and even my own sin.

Amen.

Look at the birds of the air; they do not sow or reap or store away in barns, and yet your heavenly Father feeds them. Are you not much more valuable than they? (MATTHEW 6:26)

WHAT'S IN YOUR JUNK DRAWER?

Do you have a "junk drawer"? Most people have a drawer where they keep things like clothespins, a key to a lost lock, or an adapter for plugging three-pronged extension cords into cords with only two holes. Often worse than the junk drawer is the garage or the shed.

Most people have a lot of junk they can't seem to throw away. They feel compelled to store it. Are they hoarders, or just old souls with a Great-Depression mentality? Often they don't know why they hang on to all the junk. Sometimes they just don't want to admit it.

People often feel that the more stuff they have, the more valuable their life is. They get frustrated when they see someone who has more, or nicer, stuff than they do. Or, even worse, they feel devastated when their stuff is lost or damaged—even the junk. Can you relate?

Jesus doesn't want to take your stuff away, but he does want to take away the feelings of frustration and emptiness that come along with an identity too closely attached to the stuff you have instead of him. And, if it means losing some of the things you have in order to learn how valuable God's love is for you, then have you really lost anything?

Jesus is an expert when it comes to balancing the stuff in this world with the value of his love. He was so good at it that he gave up his life so you could have life forever with him. That's how valuable you are.

Dear God, thank you for not treating me like junk. You could have put me in some drawer you seldom open. But, instead, you give me everything I need, even your love.

Amen.

Do not fear, for I am with you; do not be dismayed, for I am your God. I will strengthen you and help you; I will uphold you with my righteous right hand. (ISAIAH 41:10)

HAS IT BEEN A STRESSFUL VOYAGE?

Christopher Columbus made some great discoveries and great mistakes. He kept a journal of his voyages across the Atlantic Ocean. On several occasions he calculated the distance left to complete their journey but told his crew it was shorter than they thought. Why did he lie? He did not want them to "be dismayed lest the journey should prove long."

That's cruel! Imagine if your boss said you needed to earn 100 badges but only reported 40 when you earned 50. It's not a question of if you would be mad, but how mad you would be!

Are there times when it feels like that is how God deals with people, that he is not telling the whole truth? Have you felt like saying, "If he cares so much, then why doesn't he do something to help?"

If God says he will help and doesn't, that is cruel. But God doesn't play games using reverse psychology, and he doesn't make life really bad only to make his goodness look better. When he says, "Do not be dismayed," he means it—and he backs up his words with his actions.

He is not just *a* god or *some* god. He is *your God*. He took action to be just the God you need when he sent his Son, Jesus, to become human like you. Unlike you, Jesus has the power to overcome not only the bad and evil things in this world, but also the evil that creeps into you. He replaces your weaknesses with his strength, and his strength is so great that he came back to life even after he was put to death on a cross. But he didn't do it for himself—he did it for you.

Dear God, thank you for telling the truth about my weaknesses and the strength you give along my voyage from life on earth to heaven with you.

Amen.

Answer me when I call to you, my righteous God. Give me relief from my distress; have mercy on me and hear my prayer. (PSALM 4:1)

ARE YOUR PRAYERS A "SPAM RISK"?

Do you remember when telemarketers didn't know our cell phone numbers? Not anymore. In recent years smartphones have gotten a little smarter. Caller ID often warns: SPAM RISK.

Have you ever wondered how God feels about all the incoming prayers he receives? How can he listen to all of them? How does he choose which requests he will answer?

If you were God, wouldn't it be tempting to screen some of the incoming prayers? Maybe that thought hits close to home. While you aren't God, chances are you have felt like there are times when God has screened you. "God, why aren't you answering me!?"

Honestly, with an attitude like that, God probably shouldn't want to talk with you any more than you want to talk with a telemarketer. Regardless, when you feel distressed it's probably because things have gone terribly wrong. In fact, maybe you've experienced so much stress that you have wondered if there is something wrong with you.

At times like that, you may feel hopeless, but the reality is that you have hope because God has promised he will make things right. Best of all, he promises to make you right.

When God sees your name on his caller ID, he could say, "Wrong number!" Instead, Jesus sees your name and says,

"I better take this." Jesus doesn't just take your call; he takes everything you've done wrong and he lets it die on the cross with him. You are forgiven! So, you can call on God for help in any situation—not hoping he will hear you, but knowing he has already been merciful to you because you have heard his promise that Jesus gives the relief you need.

Dear God, thank you for making my heart right with you and mercifully answering all my prayers.

Amen.

Peace I leave with you; my peace I give you. I do not give to you as the world gives. Do not let your hearts be troubled and do not be afraid. (JOHN 14:27)

COMMON TERMINOLOGY

So you are in the middle of a disaster. It doesn't matter if a hurricane just swept through or if it is a personal storm in your life. The bottom line is that we can plan for the unexpected all we want. But the unexpected is just that. Unexpected. So here you are.

We work hard trying to prepare for the unexpected. The Federal Emergency Management Agency (FEMA) is a nationally funded agency that works at preparing for anything and everything that may happen in a disaster—an impossible task! However, there are a few principles that work in every situation.

One of those principles is known as Common Terminology. FEMA created Common Terminology so that any law enforcement, first responders, military, or volunteers can communicate effectively and work together. It doesn't matter if you have a Boston or a Biloxi accent. The words used bring meaning.

Here is more common terminology. You can find it in a book that has been around longer than our nation. It brings not only wisdom and understanding but comfort, because the language it uses has not changed.

Jesus said, "Peace I leave with you; my peace I give you. I do not give to you as the world gives. Do not let your hearts be troubled and do not be afraid."

The One who spoke those words has also not changed. Jesus speaks these words to people who are in crisis. He has been there. He has seen it. He knows what you are going through. He knows your future. In spite of that, he uses words like "peace" and "do not let your hearts be troubled."

Those words mean something. Here is a bit of clear communication for you right here, right now: Jesus stands with you. He has forgiven you. You are his. Trust him and do not let your hearts be troubled.

Dear Lord, help me listen to your promises in this time of need so that I may find the peace you have given.

Amen.

Because of the Lord's great love we are not consumed, for his compassions never fail. They are new every morning; great is your faithfulness. (LAMENTATIONS 3:22,23)

CHAIN OF COMMAND

During the middle of February 2021, a major winter storm hit Texas bringing unexpected cold. This began a domino effect of more unexpected disasters. The power went out for over five million people. The water system was contaminated. Below-freezing temperatures burst pipes and damaged homes. Without water, it was more difficult to put out fires. People struggled to stay warm.

The National Incident Management System allows first responders and authorities from different parts of the country to work together. It establishes a single chain of command. Power struggles don't work in these situations; somebody needs to be in charge so that important decisions can be made. When crisis after crisis hits, it is important to have that single chain of command.

So, you are in a crisis. Understand this. You are not alone. There is a chain of command. Although you may not see him, he put this emergency plan into place long before you ever existed for such a time as this. The proof is in the fact that the sun comes up every morning. The One who does that also continues to sustain your life.

"Because of the Lord's great love, we are not consumed, for his compassions never fail. They are new every morning; great is your faithfulness."

More than duty, it is his love for you that drives your Savior to have a plan for you. To find you. To redeem you. To take care of you. If the sun came up this morning, then you can be assured he carried out what he promised to do. He sent his Son to take away anything that stands between his love and you.

It is hard to predict what the outcome of any disaster or tragedy will be. But we know where the chain of command begins. We know that he is on your side.

Dear Lord, right now it is hard to tell if there's anyone in charge. Send me your reassurance through the hands who are working hard to help me in this time of need. Help me to see you, who is in charge and has a grip on my future.

Amen.

"Come to me, all you who are weary and burdened, and I will give you rest." (MATTHEW 11:28)

COORDINATION OF RESOURCES

Part of the problem with being in a crisis or disaster is that you are working with limited resources. Although there are plenty of resources out there, you can only access what you have ready to use when disaster strikes.

During the severe winter ice storms that hit the Gulf Coast states in February 2021, the city of Mobile, Alabama, only had five trucks available that could sand and salt roads. They were used primarily to keep I-10 open so that east/west travel would not be stopped. Minneapolis has 800 trucks.

The Federal Emergency Management Agency (FEMA) works hard to coordinate resources during disasters in order to bring what is needed to an area. Since not all disasters require the same resources, these can be shared to ensure there are enough resources where they are needed most.

You are probably feeling overwhelmed because what you are going through and the resources you have do not seem to line up. But there is One who has all you need. Jesus said, "Come to me, all you who are weary and burdened, and I will give you rest."

Better than FEMA, your Lord knows just what you need. He starts with the resource that we all lack: peace with God. He sent his Son so that we might know his love and dedication to us. His Son came to us so that we might know God is on our side through the forgiveness that comes from his sacrifice.

And his resources are limitless.

Right now, rely on those he has put into your life. Seek them out. There is help. There is hope. There is rest.

Dear Lord, right now I need many things. Thank you for giving me peace with you. Allow that peace to control my emotions and my worry. Point me in the direction for the resources that I need.

Amen.

The Lord is my light and my salvation—whom shall I fear?
The Lord is the stronghold of my life—of whom shall I be
afraid? (PSALM 27:1)

OBJECTIVE DRIVEN

Part of the difficulty in dealing with a tragedy or disaster is trying to figure out what actually has to be done to get life back to normal. The Gulf Coast saw nine named storms during the 2020–2021 storm season, which wreaked havoc almost everywhere you looked. In downtown Mobile, several oak trees more than a century old were lost. But this was not a priority.

The Federal Emergency Management Agency has set up a way to make sure what needs to be done, is done. Establishing an objective-driven plan organizes this effort. It prioritizes the safety of those involved, then the objectives that need to get done, and lastly, taking care of property.

If you are in the midst of a crisis, your head is probably telling you that everything is important. It is difficult to figure out what to do first. This is why the words from the Bible can be so freeing. Although we may not always consider it our biggest priority, our Lord tells us that he has taken care of the biggest problem in our lives. "The Lord is my light and my salvation—whom shall I fear? The Lord is the stronghold of my life—of whom shall I be afraid?"

If death is our biggest fear, the Lord has promised to take that fear away by giving us eternal life. He sent his Son to die on the cross so that we might have confidence in where we will spend eternity. If we have eternity taken care of, we can work our way back from that.

Who needs to be made safe? What needs to be done? Lastly, what property needs to be taken care of? By adding perspective to our lives, the Lord truly becomes our stronghold that anchors us through any and every disaster.

Dear Lord, thank you for putting things into perspective. Help me to see things through your eyes so that my fear is taken away.

Amen.

The LORD is close to the brokenhearted and saves those who are crushed in spirit. (PSALM 34:18)

BLAME IS FORGIVEN

As the workman came back from lunch, he saw two boys jump off the fresh cement sidewalk. One boy saw the workman and ran in the other direction. The other didn't see the man and ran right into his arms.

"Ok, bud!" the man said. "Let's go over and see what you did." Sure enough, there they were! Footprints, made by two different kinds of tennis shoes, all over the wet cement.

"He did it, mister," the frightened boy said, pointing to his friend, whose red shirt was slightly visible through a bush down the street. "Look who you are pointing at," the man said. "One finger is pointing at your friend, but the other three are pointing right back at you."

Adam blamed Eve for disobeying God, but he was guilty of the very same sin. Aaron blamed the people of Israel for the golden calf, but he was responsible for making it. Pontius Pilate blamed the Jews for killing Jesus, but he spoke the words, "Take him and crucify him!"

Covering up our blame when we have sinned doesn't make us right. We are still in the wrong, and we still deserve to be punished. King David says, "The Lord is close to the brokenhearted and saves those who are crushed in spirit." John wrote, "If we say we have no sin, we deceive ourselves, and the truth is not in us. If we confess our sins, God is faithful and just and will forgive our sins and cleanse us from all unrighteousness" (1 John 1:8).

Lord, help us admit our blame and ask for forgiveness. When we do, we find that God is just as anxious to forgive us as we are anxious to be forgiven. "The blood of Jesus Christ"—the fact that Jesus died for us—is proof that God is always ready to forgive.

Father, forgive me for all the wrong I have done.
Forgive me for Jesus' sake.

Amen.

"Give us each day our daily bread." (LUKE 11:3)

OUR LORD PROVIDES

A group of schoolchildren, playing in the snow in northern Minnesota, found over 50 birds nearly frozen. They had not flown South early enough and were now trapped by the bitter cold.

The children told their parents. The parents called the humane society. Several people retrieved the birds, thawed them out, packed them up, and sent them South by jet airplane. So the birds "flew" South. But only because someone took pity on them and rescued them from certain death.

People generally do not pay that much attention to birds. But our heavenly Father does. In his love he watches over all things, great and small. Jesus reminds us that not even the lowliest sparrow falls to the ground without our Father knowing it.

That's why Jesus tells us we should not be afraid of anything in this world, for are we not worth much more than birds? If God takes care of and feeds even the birds, surely we know that God is taking care of us and that in his love he will provide for our every need.

Jesus teaches us this truth when he leads us to pray the Lord's Prayer, "Give us each day our daily bread" (Luke 11:3). God provides for us most wonderfully with everything we need for our physical well-being. He gives us what we need, not necessarily what we want. What a gracious Lord we have!

Most wonderfully, God has snatched us from the deep-freeze of sin and warmed us with his love in Jesus. Through

Jesus' death on the cross, he has rescued us and brought us on our way to everlasting life.

Dear Father, thank you for showing us your concern over even the smallest of your creatures. Thank you for thinking of us. Thank you for giving us everything we need for our daily welfare. We are not afraid, for we know you are watching over us and providing everything we need physically and spiritually every day. What a gracious God you are!

Amen.

God made him who had no sin to be sin for us, so that
in him we might become the righteousness of God.
(2 CORINTHIANS 5:21)

IS OUR MIND ALREADY MADE UP?

A man noticed a humorous sign hanging in the drugstore: "Don't confuse me with facts! My mind's already made up!"

Many people are not interested in knowing truth, even if it is God's truth. They would rather believe what they want to believe, whether it is true or not. Their minds are made up, and nothing will change them.

The Pharisees at Jesus' time were like this. When the Pharisees questioned Jesus about himself, they were not interested in what he had to say. Jesus kept telling them he was the Son of God, the promised Savior, and that he came to do the will of his heavenly Father. But the Pharisees answered him, "You are of the devil." Though Jesus by his miracles proved that his words were true, their minds were made up.

The apostle Paul wrote about what Jesus did to save us. "God made him who had no sin to be sin for us, so that in him we might become the righteousness of God" (2 Corinthians 5:21). Jesus took our sin on himself, died in our place to pay our debt of sin by shedding his blood for us. In exchange, he has given us his righteousness. This righteousness becomes ours through faith in Jesus. We call this plan of salvation "the great exchange."

There are still many who do not want to hear or accept God's truth for our salvation. They want to make up their own minds about what they want to believe. But in refusing God's truth, they are shutting out life and salvation.

Only as we gladly listen to God's Word of truth can we know the good news of our Savior Jesus Christ, who in love gave himself as the payment for our sins. Only then can we have the joy of being forgiven and of living with our Lord forever.

> *Lord, keep my ears open to hear your truth, my eyes open to see and know your love in Christ, my mind convinced in your plan of salvation, "the great exchange," and my heart open to your plan which alone saves in Jesus.*
>
> *Amen.*

*Be content with what you have, because God has
said, "Never will I leave you; never will I forsake you."*
(HEBREWS 13:5)

JESUS IS NO RUST COLLECTION

Almost everybody has a hobby. Many people make a hobby of collecting things, such as stamps, rocks, shells, baseball cards, or dolls. However, a boy named Steve had a different kind of collection. He called it a "rust collection." He saved rusty items that he had picked up here and there—rusty nails, rusty screws, rusty chains, rusty keys.

Some people continue their hobbies all through life. But one thing is sure: it won't be long before Steve will throw away his rust collection. As he grows older, he will want to collect things that are not ruined by rust—things that will keep their value.

Many people go all through life building up "rust collections." They think the most important thing in life is to be popular, famous, or rich. They fix their whole heart on it.

But Jesus says that is foolish. He says, "Don't pile up treasures on earth, where rust can spoil them. But keep your treasure in heaven." And why? The letter writer to the Hebrews puts it this way. "Be content with what you have, because God has said, 'Never will I leave you; never will I forsake you.'"

All of our treasures on earth will last only as long as this life. They are "rust collections." But in Jesus we find real treasures that will never lose their value. In his love Jesus gives us eternal life.

Dear Jesus, let us always see you as my greatest treasure. Show us that knowing you as friend and savior is worth more than anything else in the world. Help us find our contentment in you, for you are always with us.

Amen.

Trust in the LORD with all your heart and lean not on your own understanding; in all your ways submit to him, and he will make your paths straight. (PROVERBS 3:5,6)

TRUST IN THE LORD

Trust. It's a simple concept. We learn it at a young age. Children learn to trust their parents as they are cared for by them. Little ones learn to trust their training wheels on their bike as they keep them from falling. New drivers learn to trust the brakes on their cars. As we grow older, we even begin to trust ourselves.

It's hard to do that in unexpected situations, especially natural disasters. When the unexpected or disastrous takes place, we often don't know what to do or where to turn. What's the first step to take in the aftermath of a tornado? Where does one turn when the whole town is flooded? What about dealing with the disastrous effects of a hurricane?

Instincts may kick in. Our natural response of freeze, fight, or flight initiates. Often, we turn to ourselves first. Then we may reach out to first responders or others who can offer aid and relief. Those responses are natural.

Yet, there is another option. Before anything, God tells us to trust in him. When the unexpected or disastrous takes place, "trust in the LORD with all your heart and lean not on your own understanding."

Take a deep breath. Inhale. Exhale. Then, say a prayer. You can trust God in this situation because he has been faithful in even worse situations. What could be a worse place to put our trust? Our sinful nature, which condemns us to death and hell. If we trusted ourselves, we would be doomed.

That is why God sent his Son. Jesus was able to endure the consequences of our sin. His death on the cross paid for our sins. If God can take care of that catastrophe, he can certainly be trusted with whatever other disaster we face.

Dear Lord, help me to trust in you above
all things, even when disaster hits.

Amen.

"Do not fear, for I have redeemed you; I have summoned you by name; you are mine. When you pass through the waters, I will be with you; and when you pass through the rivers, they will not sweep over you. When you walk through the fire, you will not be burned; the flames will not set you ablaze. For I am the LORD your God, the Holy One of Israel, your Savior." (ISAIAH 43:1-3)

NO FEAR

Tim was excited. His family was taking a trip to Colorado. They would spend a whole week hiking and whitewater rafting. He had been looking forward to this trip for months, and with his new gear, he was ready to go! However, when he got to the river, he saw just how dangerous it looked. Soon that excitement about rafting the river turned to fear.

Maybe you feel that way right now. You had plans. You were excited. Now all those plans and all that excitement are gone.

That is where God can help. In the passage above, he offers situations where anyone would be afraid: passing through waters, rivers, and even fire! When the water is high or the fire is hot, it's scary. Yet, God says when you pass through those scary situations, you need not fear.

Why not? Because he has already redeemed you! This past tense verb (redeemed) takes place before redemption actually happened! That's how sure God was that he would be able to take care of you. God was looking ahead to when that would happen. For us, we get to look back on when that redemption took place: at the cross of Christ. There he laid down his life for you so that your sins would no longer count against you.

God took care of the terrible situation we were in because of our sins. You can be sure that God will take care of you in the situation you are in right now.

Heavenly Father, grant me courage and
bring me through this scary situation.

Amen.

I am convinced that neither death nor life, neither angels nor demons, neither the present nor the future, nor any powers, neither height nor depth, nor anything else in all creation, will be able to separate us from the love of God that is in Christ Jesus our Lord. (ROMANS 8:38,39)

LOVE ENDURES

Has the damage been assessed yet? In situations like yours, it often feels like you find more destruction around every turn. If you haven't already, you'll soon have conversations with others about the loss they have seen too. It's a bit overwhelming.

But as overwhelming as it may be, there is another force at play that is far more overwhelming: God's enduring love for you.

In case you didn't know, God loves you—he loves you tremendously! It may not seem like it right now, but that's to be expected when you go through a disaster. And that is exactly why God reminds you of his love for you in the passage above.

With six different phrases—many of which encompass the entire spectrum of complete opposites—God is assuring you that nothing can separate you from his love. His love endures through all things, even disasters.

How can you be sure of this love? Look no further than the cross. God loved the world—a world in which you are included—and this love caused him to send his Son into the world to save it. The disaster you are facing is just one of those horrible consequences of sin from which the world needed saving. The worst consequence from which you needed to be saved is sin. That is why Jesus was sent. He would take sin on and demonstrate his love for you by dying on the cross. It's a simple yet amazing fact. Now to add to that amazing fact, God gives another: nothing can separate you from his love.

There may be a lot of damage. It may be overwhelming. But God's enduring love is greater than any disaster we can face.

Dear Lord, thank you for loving me
when I need it most.

Amen.

I can do all this through him who gives me strength.
(PHILIPPIANS 4:13)

GOD GIVES STRENGTH

Tim was frustrated. He couldn't get his printer to print. He had followed the manual and set it up just the way the instructions said, but when he went to print a test page, nothing happened. He double and triple checked to make sure everything was set up properly. It was. Yet no matter what he tried, nothing printed.

A few minutes went by and Dorothy, Tim's coworker, came in and noticed the frustrated look on Tim's face.

"What's wrong?" she asked.

"Oh, I've just been trying to get this printer to work all morning, but I can't seem to figure out the problem."

They worked together to figure out the problem, but concluded that everything appeared to be set up properly. Then, when they were about to do the test print, Dorothy checked the paper tray to see if there was any paper in it and said, "I think I know what our problem is . . ."

Sometimes, we look in all the wrong places to solve our problems when the solution is right in front of us.

You've gone through a difficult and frustrating time—much more frustrating than trying to get a printer to work. Don't look in the wrong places to get you through. God is there for you.

Often, people focus on the wrong thing when they quote the passage above. Some make it out to be all about how

_**I**_ (emphasis on "I") can do all. In reality, the emphasis in this passage isn't on us, but on God. God is the one who gives strength.

Go to God and seek strength from him. He is the source. Then, when he helps in time of trouble, the emphasis isn't, "Look at what I did!" but instead should be, "Look at what God did." God will see you through.

> *Dear Lord, I come to you for strength to get*
> *me through this difficult time.*
>
> *Amen.*

PRAYERS

In Time of Disaster

Gracious Father in heaven, your ways are not our ways; neither are your thoughts our thoughts. In your wisdom, you have permitted a disaster to cause damage and loss. Be merciful to those who are suffering. Watch over them, protect them, and graciously supply all that they need for both body and soul. Guide and guard, equip and strengthen all those who are working to help those in need and restore order. According to your will keep them from harm and bless their work. Use this difficult time to humble us all under your mighty hand, Lord. Lead us to repent from our sins and to trust in your mercy alone, for you are the only God who saves. Amen.

For First Responders

Merciful Lord, I pray for all those who are putting themselves in harm's way to assist those in need: police officers, firefighters, paramedics, doctors, nurses, government officials, soldiers, community volunteers, and all others who are working hard to relieve suffering and restore order. Strengthen them for their work, give them both courage and compassion, and bless their efforts with success. Use their work to bring relief to those who are hurting and provide order amid the chaos. Through their hands you are at work to bring many blessings to those in need, and so I give you thanks for their efforts. Amen.

For Others

Loving God, in difficult times it's so easy to focus on myself and my problems. I come to you now on behalf of others—my friends, neighbors, and loved ones who are suffering. Be with them, Lord, and if it is your will rescue them from their troubles. Help them to look to you in their distress for the comfort and peace that only you can give. Use me as your servant to help and befriend them in every bodily need and to share with them the good news of Jesus, the Savior of the world. Move me, by your selfless, sacrificial love to always put the needs of others before my own. Amen.

For Comfort

Compassionate Father, at times it feels like no one understand my needs or cares about my problems, but I know you do. Only you truly understand the depth of my heartache and the stress of my anxieties. Remind me of your promises to be with me always and to cause all things—even things that are difficult—to work out for my good. Most importantly, comfort me with the good news of my Savior Jesus Christ, who lived, died, and rose again to save me from my sins. Assure me that you will never let anything separate me from your love in Christ. In his saving name, I pray. Amen.

For Strength

God of mercy and might, I am so very weak. Recent events have reminded me how much is out of my control and how little power I have to change things. But you are strong, and you rule mightily over all things. Strengthen me, Lord, by your Word and promises. Help me to lean on you and to rely on your strength to get me through difficult days ahead. I pray this in the name of Jesus, who gave up his almighty power for a time and became a helpless baby, so that he could take my place on the cross, where he suffered and died to save me. Amen.

For Peace

Gracious and merciful God, my heart is often filled with anxiety in the present and fears for the future. The chaos of disaster increases my distress. Calm my troubled heart. Give me the kind of peace not found in this world, the peace that only Jesus can give. Fill me with the tranquility that transcends all understanding; the calm contentment of knowing that my sins are forgiven, my eternal future is secure, and that you will take care of all my needs both body and soul. Grant me peace in Jesus, my Savior. Amen.

For Patience

Heavenly Father, help me to wait patiently for the fulfillment of your promises. So often I expect you to answer my prayers in the way I want and according to my schedule. Guide me by your Word to see that your way and your timing are always best. According to your will, relieve me of my pain and suffering. But if it is your will that trouble continues for me, give me patient endurance, and help me to trust in your gracious promises. Bless me in the way that you know is best for me; through Jesus Christ, our Lord, who lives and reigns with you and the Holy Spirit, one God, now and forever. Amen.

The Lord's Prayer

Our Father in heaven, hallowed be your name, your kingdom come, your will be done on earth as in heaven. Give us today our daily bread. Forgive us our sins, as we forgive those who sin against us. Lead us not into temptation, but deliver us from evil. For the kingdom, the power, and the glory are yours now and forever. Amen.